THELONIOUS MO...

ORIGINALS AND STANDARDS

Arranged for Piano

Charley Gerard

GERARD AND SARZIN
PUBLISHING CO.
Brooklyn, New York

Cover design by Jill Hammerberg
Cover photography courtesy of The Institute of Jazz Studies at Rutgers University
Music lithography by Michael B. Hoffman

Gerard and Sarzin Publishing Co.
146 Bergen Street
Brooklyn, N.Y. 11217

Printed on acid-free paper in the United States of America.
ISBN 0–9628467–0–8 $15 softcover

Contents

Thelonious Monk: An Original — **4**

Monk's Works — **6**

Well, You Needn't — **1 0**

Off Minor — **1 5**

I Mean You — **1 9**

Ruby, My Dear — **2 4**

In Walked Bud — **2 9**

Monk's Mood — **3 3**

Epistrophy — **3 8**

Introspection — **4 4**

Monk as an Interpretive Artist — **4 9**

Stride — **5 0**

Dinah — **5 1**

Sweet & Lovely — **5 4**

Everything Happens to Me — **5 7**

Ellingtonia. — **6 0**

It Don't Mean A Thing — **6 1**

Solitude — **6 4**

Two Ballads — **6 7**

I'm Getting Sentimental Over You — **6 8**

I Surrender, Dear — **7 1**

Carolina Moon — **7 4**

Just You, Just Me — **7 8**

Final Notes — **8 2**

Discography — **8 3**

Thelonious Monk: An Original

Thelonious Sphere Monk (1917-1982) was one of the most creative figures in the history of jazz. His music is a mixture of the complex and the simple. Monk was delighted by almost inanely rudimentary melody lines and hokey old standards. The same man reveled in highly chromatic melodic lines and difficult chord changes. People accordingly responded to his music by labeling it hopelessly inaccessible or easy to like. Monk's piano playing had features of the student jazz pianist in his seeming inability to play smooth passages in the Oscar Peterson style; at the same time, his pianistics were supported by a sophistication of musical thought which helped him outdo the jazz virtuosos of the world.

In Monk the person, there was the same combination of the easy to like and the inaccessible. He was a private person whose life was restricted to his family and a few friends in his midtown Manhattan neighborhood. His wife Nellie, the central person in his life, often acted as a conduit between him and the rest of the world. Although Monk went through periods when he went without sleep and did not speak to anyone for days, at other times he was open and personable. One club owner who knew Monk in his twenties described his personality as follows:

> Monk is definitely a character. He's the type of fellow who thinks an awful lot but doesn't have much to say....He just doesn't seem to be present unless he's actually talking to you and then sometimes all of a sudden in the middle of a conversation his mind is somewhere else. He may still be talking to you but he's thinking about something else....I always used to be so disgusted with him [for being late], and yet *you never knew such a likeable guy.*

Monk's Early Years

Monk was born on October 10, 1917 in Rocky Mount, North Carolina. His parents moved to New York when he was four years old. He began playing the piano when his older sister took lessons, and Monk claimed that he "learned to read just by looking over her shoulder." Monk began taking formal lessons at the age of eleven, and formed an early preference for Fats Waller, Duke Ellington and James P. Johnson. Aspects of Monk's style go back to his teens, when he was a perennial talent show winner at Harlem's Apollo Theatre for his stride style. After developing his own style, he used stride as a sort of counter-feature to his other modes of playing. One of Monk's first jobs was with a traveling gospel group. He retained the rhythmic propulsion of gospel in his own music, although it was expressed in a style that otherwise owes nothing to gospel music.

The Forties

Monk became well-known for his performances as the house pianist at Harlem's Minton's Playhouse, one of the spawning grounds of bebop. In 1944 he made his first commercial recording as a sideman with Coleman Hawkins. In 1946 he joined Dizzy Gillespie's big band for a short while, which gave airplay to a few of his compositions. The following year, Blue Note Records contracted with him to make his first records as a leader, and the records introduced his compositions to a wider audience.

Monk's style of composing was established by his mid-twenties, a fact made clear by the dates when his compositions were first recorded. A tape recording done at Minton's Playhouse in 1941 when Monk was twenties includes a performance of "Rhythm-a-ning"; "Round Midnight" was recorded by Cootie Williams in 1944; and "Ruby, My Dear" has been said to have been composed when Monk was a teen-ager. All of the Monk compositions in this collection come from this period.

Mary Lou Williams and other musicians who knew Monk in the 1940s claimed that his distinct manner of playing the piano was not developed until after 1945. He was said to play in a more fluid manner, with occasional Tatumesque runs. Budd Johnson was one of Monk's companions at the time, and he attributed the change in Monk's style to hurt feelings over not getting any significant credit for the bebop style. Charlie Parker and Dizzy Gillespie were getting the credit which Monk rightly felt was his to share. At one point, Monk announced to Johnson: "I'm gonna let them take that style and go ahead, and I'm gonna get a new style."

The Fifties and Sixties

Although he had a consistent flow of recordings from Blue Note and Prestige in the early 1950s, Monk's career was floundering. Work began to fall off. After an unfair drug-related charge, Monk lost his cabaret identification card. Until 1966 when the law licencing club employees was abolished, performers needed the card to work in New York City nightclubs. This meant that for a time, Monk was shut out of the club scene, which was then the main source of income for jazz musicians. Furthermore, Prestige was no longer especially interested in recording any more Monk albums, preferring to concentrate on more lucrative jazz artists such as Miles Davis.

Monk's signing with Riverside in 1955 was the beginning of an upsurge in his popularity that was to culminate with his face appearing on the cover of *Time Magazine* and a recording contract with Columbia Records. At one point, his quartet featuring long-time associate tenor saxophonist Charlie Rouse was one of the most popular jazz groups in the world.

Monk composed less and less as he became more famous. On his Columbia recordings of the 1960s, Monk concentrated on re-recording his older compositions. The one notable exception was an album recorded in December, 1967 entitled "Underground," for which he composed three works: "Green Chimneys," "Ugly Beauty" (Monk's only piece in 3/4) and "Boo Boo's Birthday." Unfortunately, the hope that Monk would begin composing more was not borne out. After a couple of years in which his popularity quickly ebbed, Monk retired. A long period of near total reclusivity ended when Monk died in 1982.

Monk's Works

It is remarkable whenever a musician develops a truly original music which commands the approval of musicians from out of several different genres and, at the same time, succeeds with the public. Thelonious Sphere Monk was one of a handful of musicians who fits this description.

Coming out of the bebop tradition (indeed, an architect of the style), he was not really a bebop musician. He added qualities to bebop which were not otherwise a feature of the style. I am thinking especially of his campy spoofs, his stride left hand, and his jagged, disjunct melodies. There were the exposed dissonances, the way in which he held notes for a dramatically over-long period making them seem to float, the way he crushed notes and the way he kept one note sustained while the rest were mysteriously released.

Some Characteristics of Monk's Compositions

Monk's music is distinguished from the work of more run-of-the-mill jazz composers by his extensive utilization of motivic building blocks—blocks as small as an interval. For example, "Epistrophy" is based on the 2nd, and "Misterioso," on the 6th. A melodic segment of a handful of notes is used as the subject of extensions, transpositions, ellisions and combinations of these techniques of transmuting the material at hand. The way in which Monk skillfully makes everything in a composition grow from a single interval or a small group of notes calls to mind the work of classical composers.

Monk's compositions are incomplete without their secondary lines; nearly every one possesses passages with prescribed voicings. Leave out the major 2nds in "Hornin' In," the parallel 6ths in "Crepuscule with Nellie," or the parallel 3rds in "Blue Monk" and these compositions lose a touch of their Monkishness.

Monk had a fondness for *rhythmic displacement*: "The repetition of a...melodic segment with a different relationship to the meter in which it is found."[6] One such melodic segment is found in the first five notes of "Straight, No Chaser:" F - Bb - C - C# - D. The first note of the segment begins on *4 and*, then the segment repeats beginning on *3 and*.

A sizable number of Monk's compositions are based on the chord changes of pop standards. Although this technique of *harmonic borrowing* has been used throughout the history of jazz, it is most closely identified with the bebop era of the 1940s when hundreds of tunes were composed borrowing the chord changes of pop standards, especially George Gershwin's "I Got Rhythm."

---

[6] *The Language of Twentieth Century Music: A Dictionary in Terms*, by Robert Fink & Robert Ricci (New York: Schirmer Books, 1975).

Monk Composition	Pop Standard Borrowed
Let's Call This	Sweet Sue
Bright Mississippi	Sweet Georgie Brown
Evidence	Just You, Just Me
Hackensack	Lady, Be Good
Let's Cool One	*Bridge*, Honeysuckle Rose
Rhythm-n-ing	I Got Rhythm
52nd Street Theme	*A section*, I Got Rhythm; *Bridge*, Honeysuckle Rose
Little Rootie Tootie	*A section* (for solos), I Got Rhythm
Humph	I Got Rhythm (substitute changes)
In Walked Bud	*A section*, Blue Skies

Monk's compositions were not etched in stone, and sometimes he created several versions of the same tune. "Blue Monk" came out with a transmogrified ending when he recorded it with Art Blakey and the Jazz Messengers. "Thelonious" sounds somewhat more finished in the 1968 piano trio version than in its first recorded version of 1947 for three horns and rhythm section. Alfred Lion, who produced Monk's first recording sessions as a leader, noted Monk's mercurial approach to his compositions: "He didn't then write much of anything down....And even if he had written it down, he might have changed his mind fifteen times between the time a musician had learned his part and the final take."

Some of Monk's compositions have been better known in the manner in which other musicians arranged or recomposed them than in Monk's versions. It is not generally known that Dizzy Gillespie wrote the introduction to "Round Midnight" which has become an intrinsic element of Monk's most famous ballad. Miles Davis effectively recomposed "Well, You Needn't," giving it a new bridge with a similar melody but a different sequence of chords. Due to Milt Jackson's interpretation of "Epistrophy" on one of Monk's first recordings, the tune is often performed with a slightly different melody from the way in which Monk subsequently recorded it.

The authenticity of a few of Monk's pieces has been called into question. Jazz critic Ira Gitler states in his *Swing to Bop: An Oral History of the Transition of Jazz in the 1940s* (New York: Oxford University Press, 1985) that "Rhythm-a-ning" was taken from Mary Lou Williams' arrangement of "Walkin' and Swingin'" for a 1936 Andy Kirk recording. Idrees Sulieman claims that he wrote the first 16 measures of "Eronel," one of Monk's more bop-oriented compositions, while Sadik Hakim wrote the bridge. At the time, Lenore was a girl friend of Hakim, and the title is her name spelled backwards. Sulieman and Hakim played the piece for Monk, who changed just one note of the melody. According to Sulieman, Monk had promised to split the credits (and the royalties) but never did.

A Catalog

Monk's recorded body of work consists of 62 compositions. I have catalogued his pieces based on their earliest known recording dates.[7] His compositions fit into seven periods: the pre–Blue Note years (1941–1944), the Blue Note recordings (1947–1952), the Prestige recordings (1952–1955), the 1955 Signal recording session with Monk playing as a sideman for saxophonist Gigi Gryce, the Riverside recordings (1955–1961), the Casino recording date of 1961 and the Columbia recordings (1962–1968). A handful of titles listed as Monk compositions are actually improvised blues. These titles are: "Functional" (recorded 1957); "Bluehawk," "Round Lights" (rec. 1959); "North of the Sunset" (rec. 1964); "Blue Sphere" and "Something in Blue" (rec. 1971). These titles are not in my catalog. In addition, I did not include compositions Monk did not record such as the bebop classic "52nd Street Theme" and "A Merrier Christmas," recorded by Sphere after Monk's death.

---

[7] See Leen Bijl and Fred Canté's discography, *Monk on Record* (available from Golden Age Records in Amsterdam).

Pre-Blue Note
1941
Rhythm–a–ning
1944
Round Midnight

Blue Note
1947
Humph
Introspection
In Walked Bud
Monk's Mood
Off Minor
Ruby, My Dear
Thelonious
Who Knows
1948
Epistrophy
Evidence
I Mean You
Misterioso
Well, You Needn't
1951
Eronel
Ask Me Now
Criss Cross
Four In One
Straight, No Chaser
1952
Hornin' In
Let's Cool One
Sixteen
Skippy

Prestige
1952
Bemsha Swing
Bye–Ya
Little Rootie Tootie
Monk's Dream
Reflections
Trinkle Tinkle
1953
Friday the 13th
Let's Call This
Think of One
1954
Blue Monk
Hackensack
Locomotive
Nutty
We See
Work

Signal
1955
Gallop's Gallop
Shuffle Boil
Brake's Sake

Riverside
1956
Bolivar Blues
Brilliant Corners
Pannonica

1957
Crepuscule with Nellie
1958
Coming on the Hudson
Five Spot Blues'
Light Blue
1959
Jackie-ing
Played Twice

1960
San Fransisco Holiday

Casino
1961
Bright Mississippi

Columbia
1963
Oska T.
1964
Teo
Monk's Point
Stuffy Turkey
1966
Green Chimneys
1967
Ugly Beauty
Boo Boo's Birthday
1968
Raise Four
Consecutive Seconds

Well, You Needn't

"Well, You Needn't," like most of Monk's compositions, comes to life when the subsidiary lines intended especially for this piece are included in the arrangement. Note, for example, that in the 2nd, 4th and 6th measures of the A section Monk provided a mimicking response an octave above the melody line. The chromatically step-wise moving figure in the bass is another example of a subsidiary line essential to balancing the melody line.

The transcription of the Bridge is based on a Monk Quartet recording of the late 1960s, in which the motive begins with a major 2nd rather than the more well-known minor 2nd. Monk insisted in a 1966 Downbeat Blindfold Test that "Well, You Needn't" "starts with a Db major 9." But on the selections on which I based my arrangement, the chords are all dominant 9ths.

Well, You Needn't

Thelonious Monk

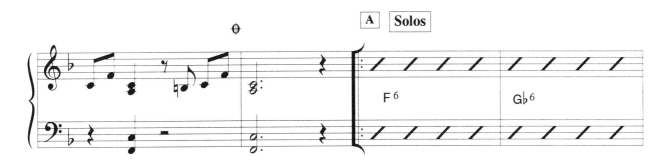

A | Solos

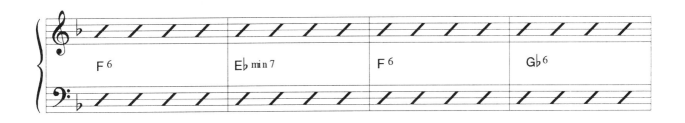

B

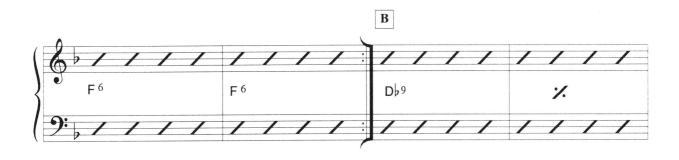

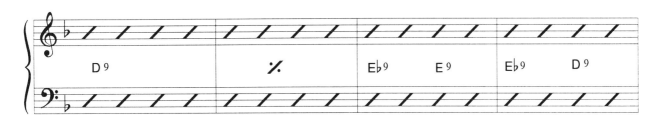

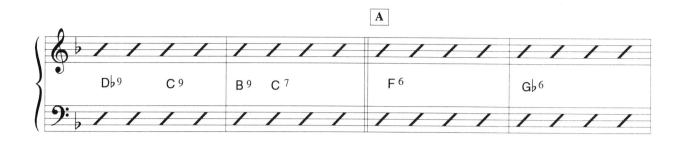

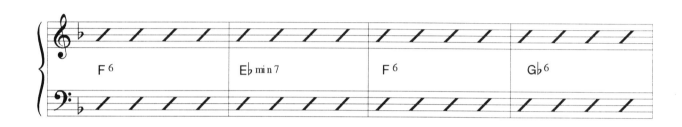

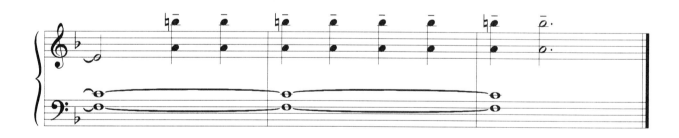

Off Minor

"Off Minor" was first recorded at a 1947 Blue Note session. My arrangement is based on the Monk–Overton big band chart written for a concert at New York City's Town Hall on February 28, 1959.

The macabre tune is cast in the traditional thirty-two measure AABA form. All of its 8-measure segments end on a D13 chord with both the 5th and 9th flatted. Monk had a penchant for this chord, and it is found in several of his compositions and arrangements. "Off Minor's" harmonic path is torturous, and it presents a real challenge to the jazz improviser.

Off Minor

Thelonious Monk

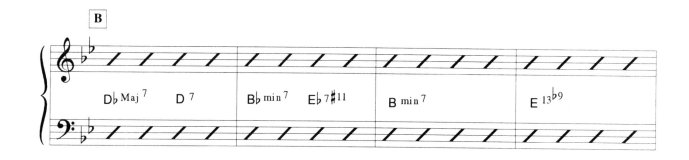

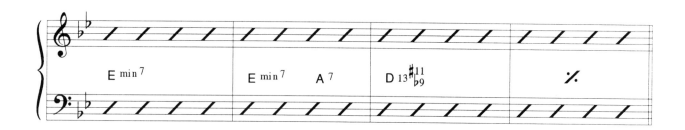

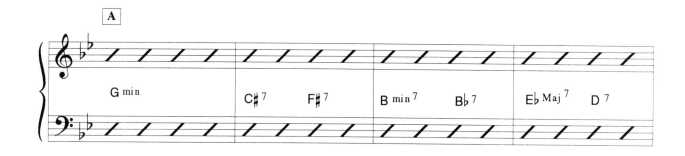

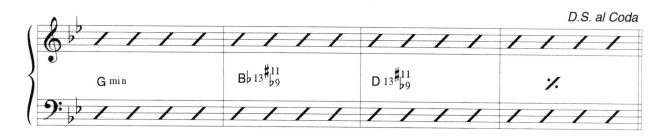

I Mean You (Stickball)

"I Mean You" was first recorded at a 1948 Blue Note session. It was heard on the soundtrack of "Straight,No Chaser," the recent documentary on Thelonious Monk. My arrangement is based on the chart Monk wrote with Hall Overton for Monk's second big band concert, which took place at New York's Lincoln Center on December 30, 1963.

The tune begins with a 4-measure passage which is repeated as a tag ending. In some recordings, Monk assigned the soloing instrument to end this passage with a G in the melody line rather than an F.

I Mean You
(Stickball)

Thelonious Monk & Coleman Hawkins

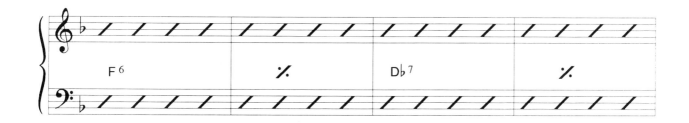

A

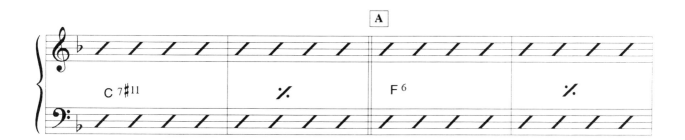

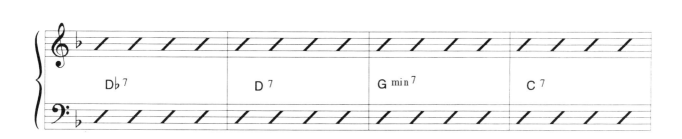

D.S. al Fine

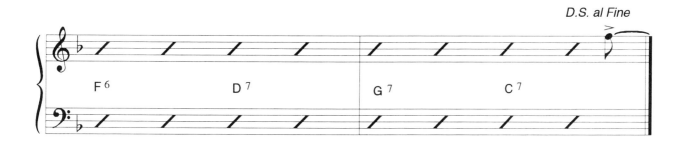

Ruby, My Dear

Perhaps Monk's most romantic piece, "Ruby, My Dear" was first recorded at a 1947 Blue Note session. In the 1950s, Monk recorded it as a feature for an early mentor, saxophonist Coleman Hawkins. The classic recording of this ballad was made with John Coltrane.

My arrangement is based on two unaccompanied solo performances recorded in 1959 and 1965.

Ruby, My Dear

Ballad

Thelonious Monk

A **Solos**

| F min 9   Bb 7b9 | Eb Maj 7 | G min 9   C 7b9 | F Maj 7 |

| Bb min 9   Eb 7b9 | Ab Maj 7 | Bb min 7   A Maj 9 | B m11   Bb 7#11 |

B

| A 6 | B min 7   E 7b9 | A 6/9   A Maj 7 | Bb 6   B°(addG) |

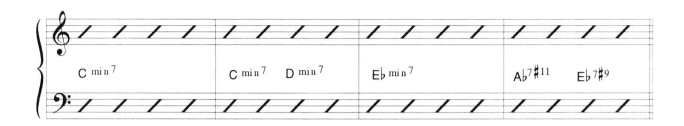

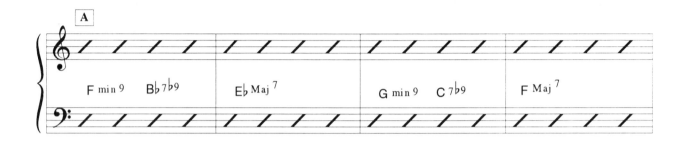

D.C. al Coda

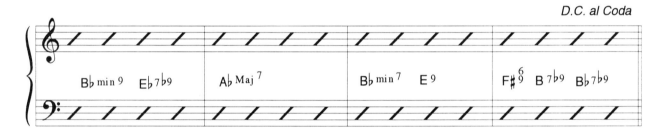

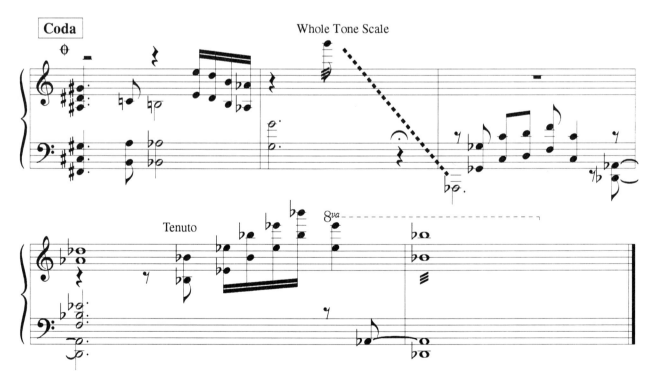

In Walked Bud

"In Walked Bud" was first recorded at a 1947 Blue Note session. The *Bud* in the title is Bud Powell, one of the great bebop pianists. The tune is in the standard AABA song form. The *A section* is based on the chord changes of the Irving Berlin standard, "Blue Skies." Vocalist Jon Hendricks added lyrics for a 1967 Columbia recording.

Monk played most of the tune in unison with the horn soloist or vocalist. He added a counter line in the *Bridge* when the melody line has a whole note. And during the first 3 measures of the last *A Section*, Monk added some echoing high C's.

In Walked Bud

Medium Fast

Thelonious Monk

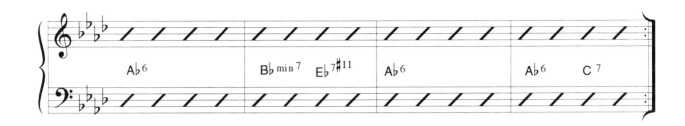

B

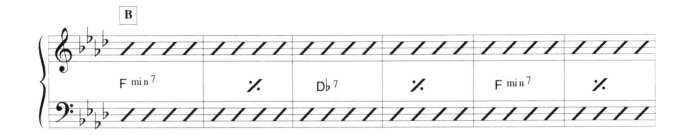

A

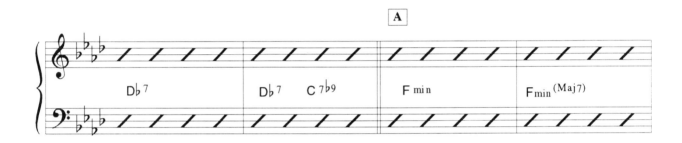

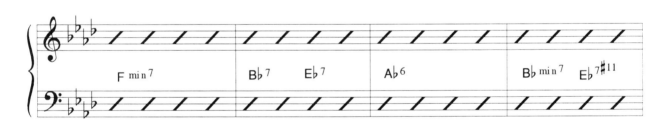

Coda

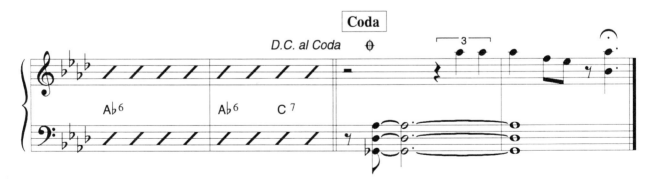

Monk's Mood

"Monk's Mood," which received its first recording at a 1947 Blue Note recording session, is Monk's most somber composition. My arrangement is a transcription of Monk's piano introduction to a big band setting of the tune, which was recorded live at Town Hall in New York City on February 28, 1959. Although the composition was written entirely in 4/4, I inserted a few measures of 5/4 to indicate Monk's performance on this particular recording.

This concert was most likely the first time that tenor saxophonist Charlie Rouse recorded with Monk. Rouse was to become a fixture in the Thelonious Monk Quartet in the 1960s.

Monk's Mood

Thelonious Monk

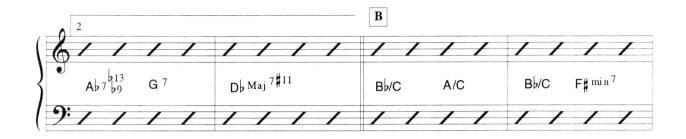

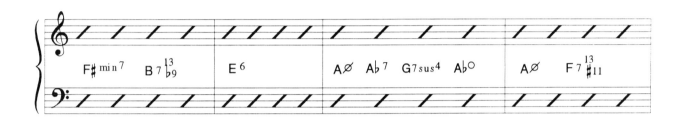

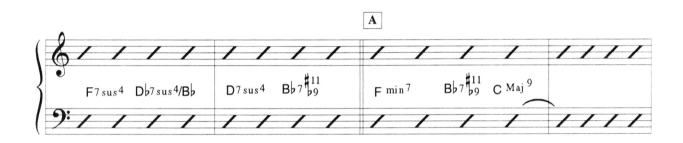

D.C. al Fine

Epistrophy

"Epistrophy" was Monk's theme song, concluding nearly all of his appearances with the piece. In an earlier incarnation it was called "Fly Right," and it was trumpeter Cootie Williams' theme song. Monk first recorded it at a 1948 Blue Note session, and went on to record it 24 times!

My arrangement is based on the Monk–Overton big band version. The melody is slightly different than in the 1948 recording, on which Milt Jackson plays the tune while Monk comps. Many musicians have learned Jackson's rendition in which the "Epistrophy" motive begins with a major 2nd, but the recordings I heard have Monk playing a minor 2nd.

Epistrophy

Thelonious Monk & Kenneth S. Clarke

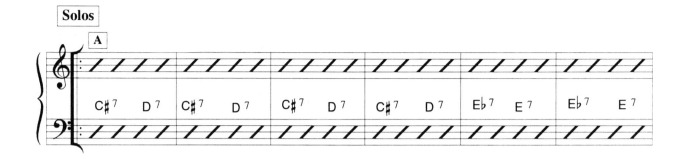

Solos

A

| C#7 | D7 | C#7 | D7 | C#7 | D7 | C#7 | D7 | E♭7 | E7 | E♭7 | E7 |

| E♭7 | E7 | E♭7 | E7 | E♭7 | E7 | E♭7 | E7 | E♭7 | E7 | E♭7 | E7 |

| C#7 | D7 | C#7 | D7 | C#7 | D7 | C#7 | D7 |

B

| F#min6 | F#min6 | F#min6 | F#min6 | B7 | B7 |

A1

| D♭9 | D9 | E♭7 | E7 | E♭7 | E7 | E♭7 | E7 |

Introspection

This intriguing theme, which seems to begin in the middle of an ongoing melody, was first recorded at a 1947 Blue Note session. Monk did not record it again until 1965. My arrangement is a transcription of the premiere recording.

The tune is 36 measures long, and is cast in the 32 measure AABA form with an extra 4 measures extending the final *A* session. Although the tune eventually finishes in the key of Db major, it lacks a tonal center.

Introspection

Thelonious Monk

Medium Fast

A Solos

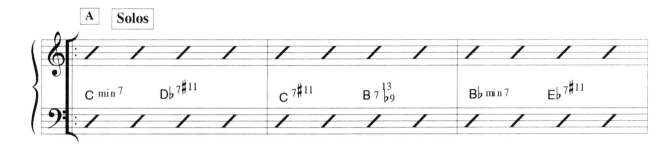

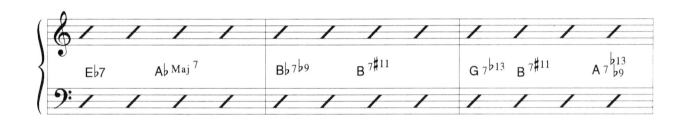

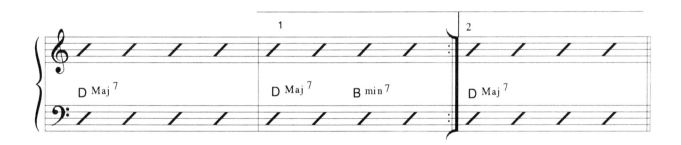

B

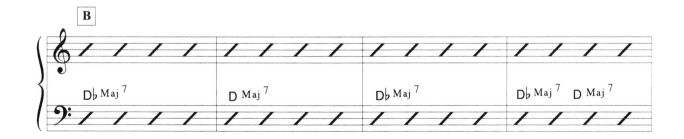

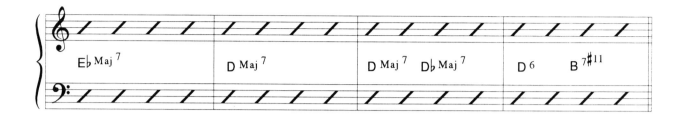

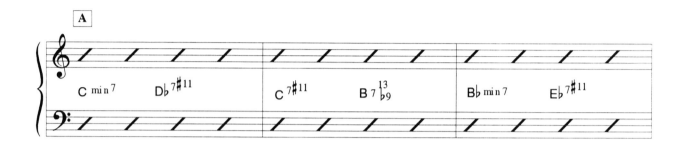

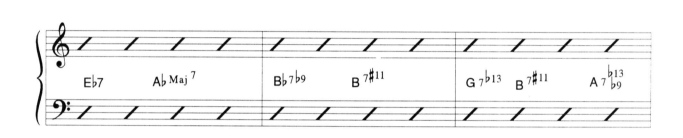

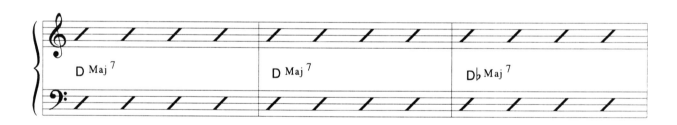

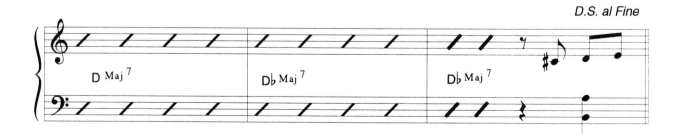

Monk as an Interpretive Artist

At one point, the idea of Monk playing pop standards was regarded as out of character. Before he joined Riverside Records in the mid–1950s, Monk had recorded a few standards on his own sessions, but his albums featured his own compositions. So Riverside's decision to begin his stay at the company with an all-Ellington record, followed by an album of old standards, was a surprise. Both of these albums helped uncover new aspects of Monk's music: his affinity with Ellington (the pianist, not the composer) and his ability to bring stride into a harmonically and rhythmically adventurous context. Later in his career, Monk gave full rein to making distinctive interpretations of 1920s pop songs. For example, one of the highlights of Monk's big band concert at New York's Lincoln Center in 1963 was his solo piano performance of a tune that few people in the audience had ever heard—"When It's Darkness on the Delta." Monk gave to modern jazz a sardonic wit and appreciation of camp in interpretations of old-fashioned, "square" songs such as "There's Danger In Your Eyes, Cherie," "Lulu's Back In Town," "Dinah," "Just a Gigolo," and "Everything Happens To Me."

Monk recorded the music of other jazz composers besides Ellington. In 1950, As a member of Charlie Parker's quintet featuring Dizzy Gillespie, he recorded several Parker originals. During the rest of that decade, Monk was a sideman for various recording sessions led by Sonny Rollins, Miles Davis, Gigi Gryce, Art Blakey and Clark Terry during which he played compositions by other jazz composers. In addition, there was Monk's 1957 recording with Gerry Mulligan in which the pianist recorded one Mulligan composition along with his own. The tunes of other jazz composers when juxtaposed with Monk compositions pale by comparison. Most lack the harmonic adventurousness, structural originality and sophistication that typify Monk's music.

In this collection, I have tried to provide several aspects of Monk as an interpretive artist. "I Surrender Dear" and "I'm Getting Sentimental Over You" feature Monk's distinctive style of ballad playing, which is marked by long fermatas (held notes) and dramatic pauses. The stride pianist in Monk comes out in full play on "Dinah," "Everything Happens to Me" and "Sweet and Lovely." Also in the collection are a pair of Ellington originals, "Solitude" and "It Don't Mean A Thing (If It Ain't Got That Swing)." The collection concludes with "Just You, Just Me"—the prototype of the well-known Monk tune, "Evidence"—and "Carolina Moon."

When Monk arranged a pop song, he sometimes had a penchant for altering it to such a degree that it scarcely resembled the sheet music version of the tune. His 1952 arrangement of "Carolina Moon" is a good example. Monk developed a new melody by speeding up the original, giving it Monk harmonies and adding a bass line. He arranged it for trumpet, two saxophones, piano, bass and drums. The recording is full of irony for at least two reasons: first, that a jazz composer considered to be in the avant-garde at the time of the recording saw any worth in such a run-of-the-mill song; and two, that it is the product of a son of the Carolinas!

Stride

Dinah

Sweet and Lovely

Everything Happens to Me

In Harlem in the 1920s a virtuoso style of solo piano came into being through the talents of James P. Johnson, Luckyeth Roberts, Willie "The Lion" Smith and others. The stride style is characterized by the constant quarter-note movement of the left hand. The stride pianist plays a single bass note on beats 1 and 3 and jumps up to a full chord on beats 2 and 4. Or s/he plays 10ths on each beat, moving in stepwise motion.

"Dinah" shows Monk the master of stride, flawlessly taking the old standard at a fast clip. His version of "Sweet and Lovely" is replete with ingenious substitute chords. "Everything Happens to Me" alternates between ballad style and a slow stride.

Dinah

Sam Lewis & Joe Young

Sweet and Lovely

Gus Arnheim, Harry Tobias, & Jules Lemare

Slow Stride

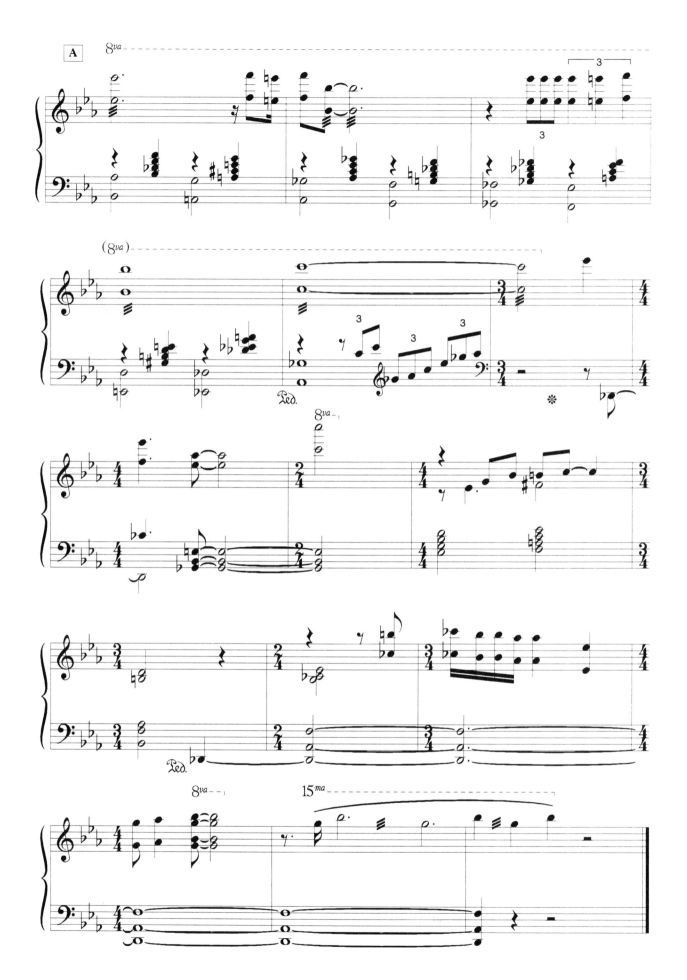

Everything Happens to Me

Tom Adair and Matt Dennis

58

Ellingtonia

It Don't Mean A Thing (If It Ain't Got That Swing)
Solitude

When Monk began recording with Riverside Records in 1955, his producer, Orrin Keepnews, decided that Monk needed to be demystified for the jazz audience. The idea was that Monk could meet his potential fans halfway by recording familiar material. The first fruit of this venture was an exemplary album devoted to the music of Ellington, from which I chose two selections.

It Don't Mean A Thing
(If It Ain't Got That Swing)

Medium Fast

Duke Ellington

Solitude

Slow

Duke Ellington

Two Ballads

I'm Getting Sentimental Over You

I Surrender, Dear

Monk, unlike other musicians of the bebop era, had a fondness for songs from the 1920s. He was especially fond of "I'm Getting Sentimental," which he recorded 11 times.

My arrangements are based on unaccompanied solo recordings. In this setting, Monk typically eschewed strict adherence to the beat and favored a *rubato* approach using held-out notes. In order to replicate this effect on paper, I disregarded the 4/4 of the originals to more precisely indicate Monk's unique rhythmic approach.

I'm Getting Sentimental Over You

George Bassman & Ned Washington

Ballad

I Surrender Dear

Ballad

Harry Barris & Gordon Glifford

A Tempo

B

Simile

Carolina Moon

Double Time Feel

Benny Davis & Joe Burke

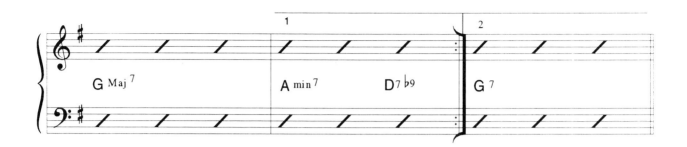

B

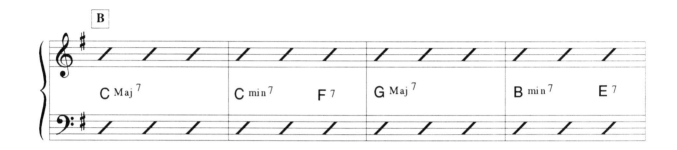

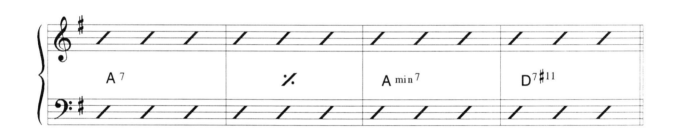

A

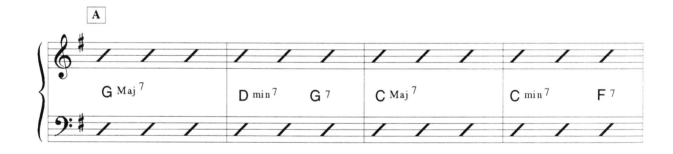

D.S. al Coda

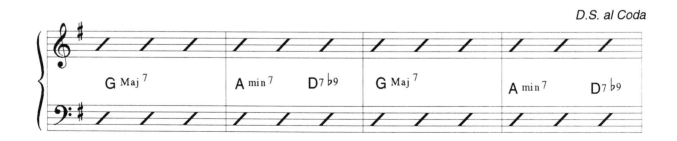

76

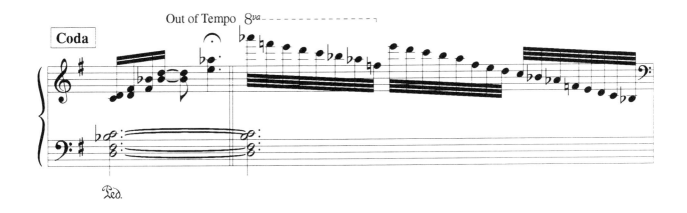

Just You, Just Me

"Just You, Just Me" developed two identities under Monk's pen: a modified version of the original melody and a new composition called "Evidence" (one time given the title "Justice"). His arrangement of this 1929 standard is in no way related to "Evidence" and stands as an entirely different artistic statement.

"Just You, Just Me" is not one of the most inspiring melodies. But Monk took advantage of its short and distinct phrases to create a subsidiary bass line. This additional line has a rhythmic and harmonic complexity totally absent from the bland melody, and sets up an imaginative counterpoint.

Just You, Just Me

Raymond Klages, Jesse Greer, & David Wolpe

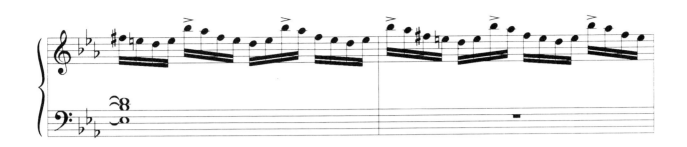

Final Notes

Thelonious Monk: Originals and Standards attempts to present his music in a more accurate and revealing light than the few existing editions of Monk transcriptions have. It is the first time that Monk's performances of pop standards have been published in a collection.

Monk was not the sort of composer who perfected a piece; instead, he was always involved in developing new versions of the same tune. My goal was to present the highlights of how he played each selection. I took features from one recording of, say, "Well, You Needn't" and added them to a transcription of another recording. In other instances, I took the *Bridge* from one source while using the *A section* of another source.

Arrangements based on jazz transcriptions always involve choices. In general, I wrote in the chord changes of the Monk originals but chose not to include the chord changes of the standards. I wrote the changes separate from the tunes for two reasons: because the chord changes Monk used in the improvisation section were sometimes a little different than in the statement of the tune; and for enhanced legibility. I wrote out Monk's introductions only when they had a melody different from that of the tune. As a result, I did not include in the selections many of Monk's characteristic introductions, which were simply an extract from the beginning or end of the tune. For my arrangements of ballads, I used meters other than the original 4/4 in order to replicate Monk's unique rhythmic feel. Unlike other books on jazz composers, this one does not include improvisations, as I intended to focus only on Monk's talents as a composer of his own music and an arranger of pop standards.

I wrote the standards as complete pieces. I did this by transcribing the first statement of the tune, followed by the concluding measures of the recording. These selections could be ideal recital pieces for classical pianists with an interest in Monk.

I hope this book stimulates the imagination of jazz pianists and composers. Monk will *always* be a timely influence for musicians who want to escape the hackneyed formulas, stylistic rigidity and blatant commercialism that afflict the world of jazz.

Discography

Carolina Moon
Genius of Modern Music, Vol. 2, Blue Note

Dinah
Solo Monk, Columbia

Epistrophy
Big Band and Quartet in Concert, Columbia

Everything Happens To Me
Solo Monk, Columbia

I Mean You
Big Band and Quartet in Concert, Columbia

I'm Getting Sentimental Over You
Pure Monk, Milestone

Introspection
Genius of Modern Music, Vol. 2, Blue Note

In Walked Bud
Misterioso, Riverside and *Underground*, Columbia

I Surrender, Dear
Pure Monk, Milestone and *Solo Monk*, Columbia

It Don't Mean A Thing (If It Ain't Got That Swing)
... Plays the Music of Duke Ellington, Riverside

Just You, Just Me
The Unique, Riverside

Monk's Mood
Orchestra at Town Hall, Riverside

Off Minor
Monk's Music, Riverside and *Orchestra at Town Hall*, Riverside

Ruby, My Dear
Pure Monk, Milestone and *Solo Monk*, Columbia

Solitude
... Plays the Music of Duke Ellington, Riverside

Sweet and Lovely
Solo Monk, Columbia

Well, You Needn't
Monk's Music, Riverside and *Monk Misterioso*, Columbia

❑ Scat! Vocal Improvisation Techniques $25

By Bob Stoloff 128 pages and accompanying CD [ISBN 0-9628467-5-9]

Learn to scat-sing! A comprehensive approach to vocal improvisation with rhythmic and melodic exercises, transcribed solos, vocal bass lines and drum grooves, syllable articulation etudes, and more. The CD, made especially for non-readers, includes call-response exercises, demonstrations and sing-along chord patterns in Latin, jazz and hip-hop styles. The author is an internationally acclaimed clinician and performer. "There is hardly anyone in the whole world who knows more about scat singing than Bob Stoloff, and this book proves it. He takes out the terror!" *Mark Murphy*

❑ Straight Ahead Jazz Fakebook $25

Edited by Charley Gerard 160 pages [ISBN 0-9628467-4-0]

"Meticulously transcribed and beautifully printed." *JazzTimes*

A collection of sixty-eight compositions written by Blue Note artists of the fifties and sixties and by young jazz musicians influenced by the Blue Note tradition. Nearly all are published in print for the first time and are not available in other fakebooks.

Sonny Clark Five Will Get You Ten ● **Curtis Fuller** The Egyptian, Sortie ● **Hal Galper** Figurine, Gotham Serenade, Loose Change, Spidit, Triple Play, Waiting for Chet, Tune of the Unknown Samba, Bop Stew ● **Dexter Gordon** Cheesecake ● **Tom Harrell** Expresso Bongo, Sail Away, Scene, Time's Mirror, Viable Blues, Upswing, Touch the Sky, Visions of Gaudi, Weaver ● **Joe Henderson** Caribbean Fire Dance, Our Thing, Teeter Totter, A Shade of Jade ● **Andrew Hill** New Monastery, Refuge ● **Freddie Hubbard** Crisis, Hub Cap ● **Bobby Hutcherson** Little B's Poem ● **Thad Jones** Let's ● **Jackie McLean** Appointment in Ghana, A Ballad for Doll, Hip Strut, Melody for Melonae, Minor Apprehension ● **Brother Jack McDuff** Do It Now, Mutt & Jeff, Snap Back Jack, Strolling Blues ● **Mulgrew Miller** For Those Who Do, Grew's Tune, Neither Here Nor There, Hand In Hand, Leilani's Leap, Portrait of a Mountain, Return Trip, Song for Darnell, Promethean ● **Hank Mobley** The Breakthrough ● **Lee Morgan** - Blue Lace, Calling Miss Khadija, Ceora, Cornbread, Kozo's Waltz ● **Duke Pearson** Hello Bright Sunflower ● **Woody Shaw** Beyond All Limits, Moontrane, Zoltan ● **Wayne Shorter** Marie Antoinette, Sakeena's Vision ● **Charles Tolliver** Right Now ● **Cedar Walton** Shakey Jake, When Love Is New ● **Larry Young** Backup, Luny Tune, Paris Eyes, Ritha

❑ Thelonious Monk: Originals and Standards $15

Edited by Charley Gerard 109 pages [ISBN 0-9628467-0-8]

"I'm sure it'll make Monk fans like me very happy." *Chick Corea*

"An important contribution to an understanding of Monk's music." *Jazz Educator's Journal*

Originals: Well, You Needn't, Off Minor, I Mean You, Ruby, My Dear, In Walked Bud, Monk's Mood, Thelonious, Epistrophy, Introspection ● **Standards:** Dinah, Sweet and Lovely, It Don't Mean a Thing (If It Ain't Got That Swing), Solitude, I'm Getting Sentimental Over You, I Surrender, Dear, Carolina Moon, Just You, Just Me

❑ Hard Bop Piano: Jazz Compositions of the 50s and 60s $15

Edited by Charley Gerard and Evan Sarzin 109 pages [ISBN 0-9628467-1-6]

"The transcriptions...are accompanied by an excellent eight-page introduction to hard bop." *JazzTimes*

Sonny Clark: Cool Struttin', Royal Flush, Blue Minor ● **Kenny Drew** Cool Green ● **Andrew Hill** Pumpkin, Subterfuge, Black Fire ● **Herbie Nichols** House Party Starting, The Third World, Terpsichore ● **Horace Parlan** Low Down, Headin' South ● **Duke Pearson** Two Mile Run ● **Bobby Timmons** Dat Dere ● **Randy Weston** Blues to Africa, Caban Bamboo Highlife, In Memory of, Zulu

❑ The Art of Jazz Trumpet - Volume One $10
❑ Volume Two $10

By John McNeil Vol. One - 64 pages [ISBN 0-9628467-2-4] Vol. Two - 48 pages [ISBN 0-9628467-3-2]

"At last! Jazz trumpet players finally have a book of their own!" *Randy Brecker*

"A *great* book!" *Clark Terry*

This series represents the first comprehensive study of modern jazz trumpet playing. Volume One contains a personal history of jazz trumpet, a selected discography and in-depth analysis of phrasing, articulation, valve technique and alternate fingerings. Volume Two consists of a variety of exercises. John McNeil is a jazz musician living In New York City. A faculty member of New England Conservatory of Music, he has made numerous albums under his own name and has appeared with Horace Silver, Gerry

Mulligan and others.

Volume One: Jazz Trumpet History: A Personal View, All In the Family—Jazz Family Tree, Jazz Articulation, Doodlin', Multiple Tonguing, Improvising Wide Intervals, Alternate Fingerings, Circular Breathing, Microphone Technique, Precision Valve Technique, Some Ideas About Practicing, The Martin Committee Connection, Selected Discography ● **Volume Two:** Articulation Studies, Cross Accents, Finger Coordination, Alternate Fingering Drills, Wide Intervals

❏ *Hip Deep* $15

A new CD from John McNeil and Kenny Berger. Brownstone Records (BRCD 9612)

To order: Send check or money order to Gerard & Sarzin Publishing Co. 146 Bergen Street; Brooklyn, NY 11217. Add $3 for shipping/handling for the first book or CD, 50¢ each additional. New York State residents add 8.25% sales tax. For further information, call (718) 858-6945. Credit card orders: Call/fax MacIntyre Music at (800) 673-3350. Visit Our Web Site at http://www.changingtones.com/gerdsarz.html.

☛*Amount enclosed (remember to include shipping/handling)*
☛*Name and Address*

Everything I play is different. Different melody, different harmony, different structure. Each piece is different from the other one. I have a standard, and when the song tells a story, when it gets a certain *sound*, then it's through...completed.

—Thelonious Monk